THE BIG SHOW

A Non-Fiction Novella

Mark Bennett

A tribute to my mentor and friend,
Television Producer, Fred de Cordova.

The Larry Czerwonka Company
Hilo, Hawai'i

First Edition – July 2013

Published by: The Larry Czerwonka Company
Printed in the United States of America

ISBN: 0615856403
ISBN-13: 978-0615856407

To my wife Mandy for her unwavering faith and making my life a joyful one.

Cover photo and design by Mike Bundlie
Text design by The Larry Czerwonka Company
Pictured are Quinn K. Rediker and Mark Bennett
Back cover photo from Mark Bennett's personal collection

Foreword

The *Reader's Digest* used to have a feature entitled, "The Most Unforgettable Character I Ever Met." If they could increase that to "The Most Unforgettable Couple I Have Ever Met," it would certainly be Janet and Freddy de Cordova, mostly because of the era in which they lived.

The pre-television Hollywood where Clark was of course Clark Gable, Bogie was Humphrey and my personal favorite, Dick was Richard Rogers, and of course, Ronnie, the 40th president of the United States, who Fred directed in the forgettable *Bedtime for Bonzo.*

Freddy and Janet were dear friends of ours and we enjoyed reading about them, and hopefully, you will too!

Bob Newhart
29 July 2013
Los Angeles, CA

Gift, n. 1. something given voluntarily without payment in return, as to honor a person or an occasion or to provide assistance; present. 2. the act of giving. 3. something bestowed or acquired without being sought or earned by the receiver.

> "Any open door that leads to a conversation that benefits you is good."
>
> ~ Fred de Cordova

I cannot pinpoint exactly the first time I saw Fred de Cordova, but I am certain I was very young, and it was a fleeting glimpse of a distinguished man sitting next to a clock and pointing to a talk show host named Johnny.

At the time, had my mother come in to tell me that it was past my bedtime for a school night, pointed to that distinguished man on my black and white Zenith television set and informed me that we would be in business together; We both would have had a good laugh.

You see, at five, I was a magician (just a short drive and we could purchase tricks from a small town in Michigan that has dubbed itself the Magic Capital of the World), at ten a classical pianist, by eighteen an actor and then on to serious studies in both crafts: First at the University of Colorado, Boulder and then on to the California Institute of the Arts. There was no Plan B.

Enter fate.

I got lucky on several occasions as an actor playing small roles on soaps, sitcoms and a couple features.

While I was on a lunch break at NBC, I went over to Studio One to listen in on Gloria Estefan and the Miami Sound Machine, rehearse.

The next day it was Bonnie Raitt performing a number from what would become a Grammy award-winning album.

The Temptations.

Stevie Ray Vaughn, on one occasion, arrived three hours before the scheduled camera rehearsal to jam with his band Double Trouble.

It was during this exclusive, aggressively loud rehearsal/jam that the Executive Producer of The Tonight Show, Fred de Cordova, cigarette in hand—yes, you could do that then—approached me.

"Excuse me," he says.

"Yes, Mr. de Cordova."

"Tell me something."

"Yeah?" I lean in, placing my still lengthy post-college hair behind my ear in order to hear without any obstruction.

"Is this good?" He nods to the band.

"Odds are favorable with the viewers."

"Very well."

And with a perfectly timed George Burns smoke-take he adds, "Name?"

I shout, "I'm Mark Bennett," and extend my hand.

"Constance Bennett, thanks for the note. I'm sure I'll be seeing you again."

That was the encounter that would forever alter what I thought was my course.

Quips turned into conversations which then evolved to the exchange of ideas and before I knew it, it was the run-ins with Fred I looked forward to the most.

I'll never be certain what it was that this universally well-respected and beloved living Hollywood legend initially saw in me. He did tell me in that first encounter that I reminded him of someone he knew a long, long time ago. My response?

"Yeah, Joan Bennett's sister," deliberately ignoring his subtext.

"That's funny," Fred would dryly say if something tickled him beyond words.

Maybe it was the quips. Maybe it was the fact that I knew his old-school references. Perhaps he liked the discreet avenue he could take by asking me questions like, "What is this Grunge nonsense anyway?"

I don't think I'll ever know. And that is just fine with me.

> "I think you are very talented, you will go far in this business, understand that I am a fan and if you don't like that you can go fuck yourself."
> ~ Fred de Cordova

I didn't know if there was a producer's school, but if there ever was an expert on the *How to's* of show business (any medium), all roads would point to Fred de Cordova. As fickle as the entertainment industry can be, fleeting for both successes and failures alike, Fred received a check every week from *somewhere* for sixty-eight years.

Tough record to break.

Florenz Ziegfeld, The Schubert's (not the organization, the brothers) Jack Warner, Carl Laemmle, Burns and Allen, Jack Benny and Johnny Carson to name a few. He knew Fanny Brice and Josephine Baker. He discovered Sid Caesar, Imogene Coca, Jackie Gleason and Danny Kaye.

Imagine then, how I felt, the first I saw on a piece of paper: "Fred de Cordova and Mark Bennett pre-approved as Executive Producers."

Or as Fred said, "You will alarm many people." Believe me, I was first in line when it came to the word, "alarmed."

There he was though, my teacher, my confidant, my partner and friend.

I was grateful for every moment.

My first day at the then, NBC Productions, was the result of Fred taking a gamble and going to bat for me. He, without my knowledge and nor did he ever bring it up anytime thereafter, basically closed the deal. Sure I had an agent, but Fred got me the office.

Right next to his.

Earlier that week, I saw him standing on *The Tonight Show* set where the monologue takes place.

Fred shouts, "Did you hear the news?"

"I'm always the last to know," I counter.

He makes a motion for me to come closer.

In an instant, all the hustle, noise and activity that go in to a nightly talk show, vanishes.

Fred quietly gestures the parameters of my deal and with typical poignancy declares, "You should be very proud of yourself. People have been walking around this town for years trying to do what you're doing right now. You have an idea, you put it to paper, and now someone is paying you to do something about that idea. You got it."

Fred opens his arms as I receive from him the biggest hug.

Then with a whisper, a look in the eye and a fatherly pat on the cheek he adds, "You should be very happy and know that I will be with you every step of the way."

A real movie moment, and when I look back, he still gave me the credit.

Kenneth Tynan once wrote: "Fred de Cordova has an engulfing handshake that is a contract in itself, complete with small print and an option for renewal on both sides."

A hug must mean you get a long life in syndication. For now, at the point of innocence, the adventure had just started.

Creative Executive . . . I always thought that was such an oxymoron. As with anything though, under Fred's aegis, I was learning the delicate balancing act between what *you* want, what the *Network* wants and what your approved production people want. All of it operating on a perceived, not-nearly-enough, so-called, shoestring budget.

Nothing rattled Fred.

And I was busy enough making my bones and staying out of the way that I had yet to achieve "rattled" let alone getting passed it.

Such an effective teacher was he, allowing me to make my own mistakes. On one particular end-of-business day, when we would have our routine *Day's Recap*, Fred, with sheer delight (when it came to controversy) told me: "I had a highly unpleasant conversation about you today with Gary Considine."

Gary was my tolerant leader in Creative Affairs and apparently I had done one of those cart-before-the-horse actions that only a good newcomer could accomplish. Instead of going to the source (me) he spared me and screamed at Fred. Gary's charitable act prevented me from therapy and gave Fred the giggles.

I was mortified which did not silence Fred's funny bone. He did however quietly explain how to repair it.

I learned you can fix chaos—but you can't fix crumbling.

> ## "You do your best to tell the truth in an industry where it's damn near impossible to do so."
> ~ Fred de Cordova

So accurate is that quote in relationship to this business of show that on many occasions it was challenging for me to utter the words, "I'm working on a couple projects with . . ."

The one truth I could hang my hat on and even *I* felt I was lying. I had yet to hit my mid twenties, I felt like I was the only wannabe actor in the world who's day job is as a producer and my evolving relationship in business is with someone who was born when Ragtime was in the Top Ten.

The fact that we were generations apart never mattered to Fred, and he always sought my opinion first before *we* made a final decision.

Fred approached business in a very step-by-step manner. Knowing that television is a series of your best-educated guesswork, he always wanted to look at the downside first. He spoke simply without being condescending and felt that redundancy or repetition kept everyone on the same page. He was fair but always favored the Network. He felt that there was an art to what he would call "staff casting." In other words, you hire according to the needs of a particular show. "The toughest part of your job as an Executive is saying 'no' to your friends . . . This is why I don't have any."

He was an appropriate gambler. An optimist. A mensch.

He had the wonderment of a child. He was selfless. He could effortlessly give off the impression that he was thick-skinned. He was ageless. He kept up with the times even though he may not have liked it. He was a smart-ass, the best audience in the world, and he was always full of mischief.

During the beginning part of my "tenure" as a member of the organization at NBC I found it no coincidence that my initial Talent obligations where I was required to sell-in-the-hopes-of-booking certain individuals all happened to be none other than . . . Fred's friends.

Smart and safe.

It honestly didn't matter to me although I always imagined Fred having dinner with these people the night before: "I'll have Mark give you a call tomorrow at home and you respond as if you've never heard this before."

Nevertheless, I was having a particularly productive day—

"Hello Mark? Jack Lemmon. How are ya?—"

When it became necessary for me to make a mad dash to the restroom in between phone calls.

As I stand there, doing what one does, I overhear a flush from the stall next to me.

While I am thinking of the calls I have to make, I feel a gentle but firm push of a hand.

And with a, "Did you miss?" Fred de Cordova was out the door.

Words of gold. All the more reason to try and *not* use his name.

Corporately speaking, I was nowhere near being in the clear. A good indication of just where I stood was the fact that to meet with my superior, I had to go through the formality of having my agent book it. Odd, since his suite was right next to mine. Fred could just walk in.

Exactly.

Even so, I still received the Producer's only fan letter which always begins, "Pay to the order of . . . ," thanks to my eye-rolling boss.

So, as we had done before, Fred and I are seated across from our Creative Superior. This time, I noticed our pitching has developed a type of Ping-Pong. We are beginning to anticipate what the other is going to say. The producer's jazz. I really liked how it was all going. Then Fred, to make a point, made a reference using the classic Samuel Beckett play *Waiting for Godot*. What a clever and astute way of describing this, I thought.

Gary looks at us in disbelief.

"Waiting for Godot? What the fuck is Waiting for Godot?" he says.

There was a brief silence.

"Nothing to be done," I parody to Fred.

"I'm beginning to come to that conclusion," he counters, quoting the second line of the play.

And with that, Fred grinned and we left. Quickly.

> "It is important *not* to have a meeting before you decide to do something."
> ~ Fred de Cordova

It wasn't long before a shift started to occur within the organization. Todd Leavitt, the Business Affairs man who facilitated my deal with Fred was moving on. Gary Considine was changing capacity into a bigger and better new deal. Many changes were happening, and I had the clever/stupid thought of changing from an independent contractor to having a living, breathing company and as an owner I wanted to see what Fred's thoughts were on the subject.

Without question, Fred defied all logic. He was in his eighties and even though he had a truckload of laurels, he wasn't about to consider resting on them. That being said, even though nothing would please me more than to have him nearby, he still had been with NBC for over twenty-three years. Who was I to uproot him?

I knock on his always open door and peek in. "Talk," he says.

"Fred . . . uh . . . there are a lot of changes going on . . . uh . . . and"

I stutter and stammer my way through until finally: "Stop. Start over."

(Fred artfully would do this so that the *requester* could gather thoughts and execute more efficiently and with *word* economy.)

"I want to run a company so that we could have a shot at owning a larger percentage. Oh, and I want you to do it with me."

An eternity passes.

Fred takes a puff of his cigarette. "Where should we go first?"

Fred smiles. I leap. I jump with "thank you's" and a "this is so great," and I start to make a b-line around Fred's desk to give him that Big Hug.

Over my shouts Fred deadpans, "Jesus Christ, you can't contain yourself. You are disrupting the other offices. Now you're going to jump all over me for chrissakes. Probably blow in my ear. My God, you're slobbering all over me—"

By this time, I'm laughing and making my way out the door.

Just as I cross the threshold I hear, ". . . although I think I kind of liked it."

Enter Nightingale Productions, Inc.

"*Johnny Came Lately* and Mark came after that."
~ Fred de Cordova

There is no such thing as an independent producer. Co-dependent I believe is accurate.

That said, I have learned that it is practical to view running any company let alone one in television, the same as running a greenhouse. One has to maximize their efficiency so that there are plants growing in every square inch of growing space. And if you want to bring something to market next Mother's Day, you'd better seed last week.

So, one does a delicate dance between television's two very distinctive industries: The Development Business and The Production Business. Sometimes you hope the twain meet. It is possible to make a modest living and stay in Development and that may have been helpful in bridging some gaps, but with Fred, obviously, he increased the odds as an insurance policy of sorts so that we could perhaps pay a visit and make an appearance (with better profits) in The Production Business.

Frequently, I would express to Fred that it was one thing to know you're lucky in retrospect and quite another to know it as it is happening. He in turn, in his typical self-deprecating way would say that *he* was the lucky one.

Also unusual (or maybe not so unusual) was the fact that Fred was quick to note that at least internally in this industry, the focus would be on me. He said, "When you're in the cat-bird seat, the downs far outweigh the ups. So what time would you like me to show up tomorrow morning, Boss?"

Truth really is stranger than fiction. Then again, I've heard that it is always good to hire people who can do your job far better than you. . . .

I felt so fortunate. My infant company growing into a toddler.

While we "planted seeds," I had a flashback. When I was a kid, I watched my parents start with nothing more than a card table, a phone, my mother ran the printing press (she still winces at the memory of ink under her nails), and my father did the sales calls.

They broke even in a year, put me through college and had a great twenty-one year run.

Dad would say, "Running a company means you're the one who opens the door, cleans the toilets, recognizes that sometimes meeting payroll is a victory unto itself, always pay yourself last and finally, (and this has always been his belief) if you want a company to run well . . . hire women."

That last part would make someone in Human Resources cringe today, but there's a lot of truth to what he said, and I'm glad there is a thing called osmosis.

My Dad's example, combined with my observations of the well-oiled machine called Carson Productions, helped to expand Nightingale.

(When I asked Johnny Carson how many people worked on The Tonight Show staff, I remember his answer, "'Bout half.")

So, with a shift in thinking, Fred and I began looking outside the walls of NBC Productions (still giving NBC first choice, of course) paying closer attention to the sensibilities and personalities of the other networks and by so doing, expand Nightingale Productions' contact pool.

Good ideas change cultures.

I believe in what I call the Producer's Cosmos. That is, that ten producers can come up with pretty much the same idea around the same time and the person with the most energy wins.

I also believe that every producer has a total bomb of a show that will never get on the air that they are just itching to do.

Then, there's a third belief in which, due to the odds that are against you, the experience (almost) outweighs the result because every producer should love the process.

Then once in a great while, when the planets are in the right place, and it is somewhere around 72.4 degrees with a light breeze, the producer gods kiss you on the cheek and present you with something fully realized, utterly simple, original yet familiar, an idea that travels well, has broad appeal and gets the heart pumping by the most jaded of network executives who has heard the best and the worst ten times over.

Lightning struck, and I pitched Fred de Cordova. He saw what I saw.

It was magic.

"It is the most original idea I've seen cross my desk in many, many years," Fred declares.

"Let's take this all over town," says Youth.

"No, we need an organizational okay. We need funding for a ninety day period to corral celebrities, and to see if we're genuinely onto something."

Oh that's right, Fred always says that any good Producer does not put dollar one of his own money into any project.

"That makes sense," I say.

"We'll take it around when we're sure," Fred continues, "It is my belief that three months is a realistic time frame at which time we can determine whether or not to commit and/or exploit this elsewhere."

Fred lights a cigarette.

He continues, "We'll set this up as a Special, which could lead to a weekly show. Weekly makes it sound too easy."

NBC thinks it is too much like a previous Special. Fred, always quick on the uptake, "It is 180 degrees the opposite, and this is why."

NBC on a second thought adds, it is too *PBS*.

I mention to Fred, "We need to take this outside."

Fred grabbed the phone and called Garth Ancier, then President of the newly established WB Network.

This would be the first time Fred and I pitched outside the confines of NBC, and I couldn't be more nervous.

Then it had occurred to me, when was the last time Fred pitched outside NBC and who was he with? Jack Benny? George Burns?

At the time, this thought did not help my already existing nerves.

I remember I thought, "Is this leap-out-of-the-comfort zone, my fault?"

Then, "This man next to me is sure going out on a limb."

(I'll never know the half of it.)

Funny thing, is that later that day I had an opportunity to be of service for the Talent at an APLA benefit concert. Elton John, Joni Mitchell, Nona Hendryx, George Michael, Clint Black, of course— Little Richard; a real high-end concert that Bernie Taupin put together. Normally, this would be exciting. Frankly, it paled in comparison to the (likely) twenty minute, ten o'clock pitch meeting I was to participate and lead.

My face was flushed the moment I got up that morning and one would think I had lockjaw due to my clenched teeth.

I agonized, "I am two steps away from an anxiety attack because of a pitch meeting?"

My resolve: Excellent. *This is good.*

Fred was not much on waxing nostalgic. For him it was about today and how is that going to affect tomorrow. But at that moment, as we drove onto the WB Network lot and passing the guard, Fred reminisced, "The first time I was on this lot, it was as a Dialogue Director in 1942 for the motion picture *Mildred Pierce*. Joan Crawford won the Oscar that year."

This is the one time when you wish you had a longer drive.

The meeting came and went. Garth was gracious.

On our way back to the car, the first words uttered were from Fred when he whispered, "Now tell me, how do you think the meeting went?"

I told him my thoughts and he replied, "Yes. I would agree with that."

That was the first time I felt like a partner but I could never really say that. Ever.

> ## "The next best answer to a yes is a no."
> ### ~ Fred de Cordova

That doesn't mean you have to *like* the "no." Which is exactly why Fred *may* have had an Iago-like conversation with a certain Boss's Boss back at NBC to perhaps re-investigate a potentially viable idea.

We met with Gary Considine.

The working title of this idea was simply and generically entitled, "The Program."

Two days, six hours and twenty two minutes later Fred calls with a heavy tone of disappointment.

"We have a real roadblock. Gary says it's star driven, too booking intensive to proceed. I wanted you to know as soon as I found out . . ."

I told him that it sounded like good news to me, that perhaps it could be looked as a buying sign and that maybe Gary wants us to find a solution to a potential problem.

"I'm not sure if there's a way around this one." That evening, on the way back to my car, in between NBC's main building and what's called, "The Catalina Building," on a skinny little path, who should be coming in the opposite direction but Mr. Booking Intensive himself. Time to bring up the subject, hit him with a rebuttal, make it count, seize the day and at the very least, get another meeting out of it.

Score.

I called Fred. He asked me to repeat the conversation again and then he reiterated my conversation back to me.

"You did an exceptional job, now go to bed," Fred exclaimed to make tomorrow happen sooner.

The next day, a voice mail from one Mr. de Cordova who had the kind of excitement that only a true salesman has on the eve of a possible buy.

"I was happy because Gary approached *me* about bumping into you and told me that we will all meet on Friday. What you said last night impressed me and that event never happens."

Friday came. Result?

To justify paying us a nickel, it was my job to create a wish list/show over the weekend, and then submit it to Gary on Monday morning.

I drew up a show as well as an alternate show. Fred's only comment that Monday morning was, "I wish this was on tomorrow night."

We got the nod to move forward.

> ## "Top-Flight Talent is in the eye of the beholder and never have your heart set on any one of them."
> ~ Fred de Cordova

We had a finite period before our option on this project was up.

We hustled, made calls.

Fred is quick to check in, "Aren't you excited? I'm so proud of you. Knowing this business as I do, I know how difficult it is. You surprise me with all this consistent movement."

"I just want to get you another Emmy, that's all."

At this point we also decide to alter our working title in order to incorporate the hook. In other words, "Tell the audience ahead of time what they're about to see."

I however didn't want to give too much away.

For now, the show will be known as, *Tonight's Unlikely Program.*

(A definitive middle-finger wave of defiance to the fates.)

And it makes people laugh.

Interest with Talent was high.

Network interest was low.

While I was more than a little frustrated at our perceived lack of enthusiasm on the Network side, Fred pointed out, "If they were excited and *got* what we're trying to do, then they'd all be wonderful people. Remember that."

Even so, this NBC step deal (which means, by the way, "We're not really sure whether to have faith in your program or not.") was beneficial for us to validate what we thought would be a viable property.

On March 29th 1995, a surprise fax came into the office.

The company letterhead said: *Grace Under Fire* and we were carbon copied.

Here is what was written:

Dear Warren,

Although I haven't met you, writing this to you seems to be a very good way to confirm my interest in performing on *Tonight's Unlikely Program*, the show created by Mark Bennett and Fred de Cordova. One of the ways I can get out from underneath the "hot house flower" syndrome of a comedian starring in a sitcom is to do a scene on a show like this. Actually, that phrasing might not be correct—I've never seen or heard of a show like this. Please accept my kudos, in advance, for producing something so unique that it qualifies as exciting in every sense of the word. Thanks for your time.

And, by the way, isn't it nice to get a letter from a celebrity who's not asking for money?

Sincerely, with warm regards,

Brett Butler

At the time, Brett Butler had a top ten prime time television show ON ANOTHER NETWORK. Let me repeat, ON ANOTHER NETWORK. Pretty gutsy and kind of her to take it upon herself and throw in her two cents to the President of the Entertainment Division in support of our budding idea. I swear I saw a tear running down Fred de Cordova's cheek.

As the option period grew near and we were second-guessing that perhaps NBC would not renew, we began focusing our energies to see if we could engage the other Networks.

"I believe in this Project because I believe in you."
~ Fred de Cordova

Personally, the thought of our show being on CBS excited me. The Tiffany Network, Black Rock, Bill Paley, Ed Sullivan, Carol Burnett and it was historically significant for Fred; Benny, Burns and Allen . . . there were so many reasons.

I thought ABC was interesting. It skewed young, as they say, but also to Fred, having been around so long, this was still the *New Upstart Network*.

At the time, I figured it would be best to do the preliminary meetings myself and if it turned into something more substantial, then Fred would join in.

This was definitely the equivalent of walking a tightrope on a few different levels.

First, the two biggest mergers thus far in Entertainment (Disney/Cap Cities/ABC and CBS/Westinghouse) were announced.

Second, for me, both networks one could say were *cold calls*.

Third, Nightingale needed another deal in the till. Fourth, anything I said or did would in turn be an immediate reflection on Fred de Cordova.

No pressure at all.

The one difference this time though, is we were one step beyond nifty idea and had a stack of letters of intent to peddle from a diverse pool of talented celebrities.

"Go get 'em."
~ Fred de Cordova

I have a recollection of a time when I was six or seven and I would prepare for a social event, let's say for the first time without my parents, my mother's line would usually be, "Now you are representing The Bennett Family, so mind your manners, be polite."

You get the picture.

Well, no difference here, I'm just older.

I pitch ABC's Sr. VP of Specials, Mark Zakarin. Not a bad fit but he said he would not be ready for five months.

The President of HBO is an instant "no."

I pitch the Director and VP of Specials at CBS and left feeling encouraged.

My agent will follow up at CBS.

Fred calls golfing friend and President Peter Tortorici at CBS.

I am constantly keeping in mind that the deal to make is the deal that gets the money back first.

Peter Tortorici leaves CBS.

I'm also thinking that timing is everything.

Les Moonves moves in as the new President of CBS Entertainment.

Fred calls Les Moonves.

Mr. Moonves recommends, "Have your guy call the VP of Operations and Planning and make sure your guy tells him that *I* told him to do it."

Fred immediately calls me.

I book the meeting.

Also in attendance is the Director of Scheduling and Programming.

Agent follows up.

My answer comes back via the VP of Operations and Planning in which he states, "It's just not special enough. Not a real ratings grabber."

I couldn't resist, "Well I understand that perhaps we're coming from an NBC sensibility but it is my belief that we're flexible enough to tailor suit the show to fit CBS's needs, wouldn't you agree?"

"I'll have to get back to you on that."

Later that week, while at CBS on another matter, I see Les Moonves and the new Vice President, Billy Campbell. I thank them for giving us an answer quickly and how much we sincerely appreciated that.

"Answer for what?" They indicate.

"Fred de Cordova and I pitched a show and we got the final word on it. We just appreciated the quick response. So, I just wanted to say, Thanks."

"What show?"

A couple days later I phoned Billy Campbell and asked if I could give him an opportunity to pass on the show that they have yet to hear.

Graciously, he told me he, ". . . knew what it was like," and granted me the meeting.

Although happy with the reception, I personally thought with all the significant changes going on at CBS as well as the ones that *will* happen internally, the timing probably wasn't the greatest. But then again, what do I know?

"Morale is pretty low around here," Billy comments.

"That happens," I respond with support.

"People are afraid. Les and I are trying to get to know as many people as we can. A lot of people are complaining about some of the internal decisions made by Les," Billy says with a sigh.

"It's like this," I say as I make my way out the door, "The first thing you do when you get on a horse and you know how to ride, you have to spin it around a couple times. People are complaining because they perceive they are the ones who are shoveling the shit."

Back at our offices, Mark Zakarin from ABC calls.

"Pitch me the show with a clean slate as if I have never heard it before," he says, "I'll have John and Ted with me."

"Great, I'll bring Fred," I tell him.

"It's not dead yet, kid."
~ Fred de Cordova

It is the morning of our ABC meeting. We are to meet with Mark Zakarin, his colleague John Hamlin and their boss (and President) Ted Harbert.

We quietly await our limousine at NBC.

"What time is it?" Fred asks.

"Ten twenty-eight."

"ABC is on the other side of town, we better not be fucking late."

The car pulls up.

The driver jumps out.

"Mr. de Cordova, Mr. Bennett, I'm sorry—," the driver opens the door.

"You're late. Just fucking get us there," Fred says with the utmost diplomacy, getting in first.

I enter and the door closes.

Fred reaches in his breast pocket and pulls out his cigarettes, "Would you like one?"

(Now smoking is bad for your health, but this is the one and only time I was glad I knew how to smoke because had I coughed on the first puff, Fred might have seen this as a defect of character.)

"Sure, thank you."

As we make our way around Warner Bros., I get another cherished peek at my mentor's past.

"When I did *Hellzapoppin'* with Danny Kaye in 1935"—

This is great I am thinking when I happen to notice the driver is taking us on what I feel is the long-way-around-the-barn route.

"Excuse me Fred," I reluctantly stop him, "Any reason you're not taking the canyons?" I ask the driver dripping with subtext.

"I thought we'd go down Highland and hang a right on Santa Monica."

"Jesus Fucking H. Christ," comments Fred.

"How long have you lived here?" I ask, reaching for status quo.

"A week, but I have a Thomas Guide."

The driver isn't winning too many points.

"Shit. We've got twenty minutes before we're considered late," I announce.

"Christ."

"Shit."

What's that expression about cutting the air with a knife?

"Well," Fred chuckles, "Would you like another cigarette?"

The one blessing out of this unfortunate choice from the driver is as we sat there, Fred realized that it had been a while since he had been in this part of town. He would point out various landmarks that are still standing as well as the ones that are merely a part of Hollywood's collective mind's eye.

"Mocambo used to be there. Great flaming martinis," Fred smiles at the memories and then points to an oncoming studio on our left, "I directed Elvis Presley there. Very, very sweet polite young man," then adds, "A lot like you, I think."

How many times has someone said to you, "You remind me of this friend of mine" or, "You gotta meet so-in-so, you guys must have been brothers in another life," and you don't think anything of it?

With Fred, it's Elvis Presley.

Or, "Ava Gardner would have loved you. [You are] Completely her type."

Or, "Clark Gable would have said exactly the same thing. I think you and he would have liked each other."

Fred exhales and adjusts his window, "Over there is where I first met Duke Wayne," and laughs as I start to think this is better than what we're about to pitch, "Lovely man, except for he would get very mean when he was drunk."

In an obvious parody, I point to our right, "Hey Fred, there's The Troubadour. That's the place where John Lennon and Harry Nilsson got thrown out for heckling The Smothers Brothers."

"I wasn't there that night."

After a couple twists and turns, a missed exit and more shouts from the back, we finally arrived at ABC with two minutes to spare.

My door opens.

"I'm sure glad we made it on time," says a relieved driver.

"Fuck you," Fred mentions.

You never really knew where he stood on a particular matter.

I tipped.

Because I knew the journey is what I would remember the most.

"Most things fail. Most books, most albums, most films, most television shows and even some really good ideas. Don't lose sight of your hopeful result but don't focus on it. Remember that."
~ Fred de Cordova

We stand in the middle of the lobby at ABC Entertainment.

"You know, I had one of my most tactless moments in business with one of the gentlemen we're about to meet. Many years ago, when he was an Executive at NBC . . ."

And with that, Fred tells one of those I-knew-something-that-was-going-to-happen-to-him-before-he-did-and-brought-it-up stories about this guy I'm meeting for the first time.

Lovely.

"I hope," Fred concludes, "He's forgiven me by now."

Enter Anxiety.

An assistant asks us to follow her.

Walking down that hallway—every office from floor to ceiling is smoked glass—Fred casually strolls, nodding and saying hello.

Yeah, I'm with him.

The first one I see is Mark Zakarin with a look on his face that seems to say, "If you can get Fred de Cordova anywhere outside NBC by eleven o'clock, I think you'll be able to pull this whole show off."

"It is a real pleasure to meet you Mr. de Cordova, c'mon and meet an old friend of yours."

Mark Zakarin smiles, shakes Fred's hand and pats me on the back excitedly.

I feel just a thousand dollars shy of a million bucks at this point.

We enter an office to meet John Hamlin who greets Fred with a big hug commenting on how much of a mentor Fred has been.

"Just as John has been a mentor to me," Mark interjects.

"It must be contagious," I say.

A laugh, and the meeting begins.

Forty-five minutes later, John Hamlin states while messaging his forehead, "Fascinating idea. There needs to be some retooling..."

I can't say I'm particularly fond of that word.

"Of course," Fred validates.

"We can work it out," says a grinning-from-ear-to-ear Mark Zakarin.

"Mark," John Hamlin looks directly into my eyes, "We don't know you, and we don't know what you know but whatever you don't know, we're here to show you."

Quick let's end the meeting before they do.

With the grace of a ballet dancer and a beautifully executed concluding statement: Fred de Cordova closed my folder filled with paperwork I had planned to disperse, I quietly and discreetly inserted it into my briefcase; we stood up, we shook hands and got the Hell out of there while the feeling was still very positive.

Back at the car on our way to NBC, not much was said.

"Next week I'll pitch this thing at FOX just to make sure we've covered all the bases," I break the silence.

"Good, let me know how it goes."

"A Network that's not nervous is not in this country."
~ Fred de Cordova

FOX is an immediate "no."

ABC's Mark Zakarin calls and wants to retool it for the '96-'97 season.

I call Fred who wants "holding money." I tell him we should try and hold off bringing that up.

An agent from the illustrious Creative Artist Agency calls with the immortal words, "What can we do for you." I had him follow up at CBS and ABC.

I ask Fred to have a conversation with Billy Campbell at CBS, "I'm really proud at how you are handling all this," my teacher tells me.

ABC asks me to book a meeting next Thursday and ". . . make sure it's a half hour."

Fred calls, "I'd be happy to make another call to Billy Campbell (at CBS) but I will only do so on your word."

Why does that somehow sound backwards?

At the conclusion of ABC's meeting, Mark Zakarin confides, "You're almost there. The show is almost ready. The Talent is great. Music choices are great. Minimal adjustments and it will be ready to buy."

That evening Fred reflects, "We've been through a lot together, you and I."

It's a good thing we only can see one day at a time.

After said "adjustments," I am back at ABC on a cloudy day in October on the 16th. Mark Zakarin and I are here to talk about final terms before he proceeds for a full Creative sign off.

Upon showing Mark the revisions, he says, "I am proud. I'm really impressed. You have done a phenomenal job. Now, ABC will issue a licensing fee to Nightingale Productions. It will be between seven hundred fifty and nine hundred thousand dollars."

"Sounds doable."

"You are pre-approved as Executive Producer and Fred will be Co-Executive Producer."

"No *Co*, get rid of the *Co*."

"Alright," Mark smiles and makes a note with the pencil in his hand.

"Something tells me you should change my title to 'That Guy'."

The ABC Executive winks and then, "Oh and I assume you want to own the show?"

"Sure."

(You know, one can be a part of so many projects over the years but it is rare to hear those words and with a simple stroke of a *pencil*, the only word I could muster was, "Sure.")

"Alright then, I'll take this up the flagpole and let's see if we can't get this thing going. Anything else?"

"Uh, yeah."

"What's that," my fearless leader gets up from his chair.

"Will the check clear?"

And with a laugh, a hug and a kiss on his assistant's hand, I head toward the lobby. As I enter, I see Dick Clark walking in. He sees me, does his trademark salute and goes on his way.

Now that's a good omen.

In the middle of this bustling lobby I pick up the phone to tell Fred.

One week passes and I receive word from Mark Zakarin that the meeting with the President is today and that John Hamlin signed off on it.

My wise mentor suggests, "Take a sedative."

On Wednesday, October 25th, 1995 at 9:30 a.m., Five months to the day that Mark Zakarin said he would be ready, ABC bought *Tonight's Unlikely Program*, a series of one-hour Specials to be aired in prime time.

I tell Fred, "Now the work starts," irony intended.

"God bless us all," he responds adding, "One more thing."

"What?"

"I hope you understand something."

"What's that?"

"They really aren't buying the show."

What?

"They're buying you."

> ## "We will try our best not to fuck this up."
> ## ~ Fred de Cordova

"How fast can you get down here," Mark Zakarin urges.

"I'll leave now."

"Now remember," Mark adds, "We're brothers in this. No more selling."

"Alright, sure."

I make the fastest drive to the company that at this time refers to itself as "A, Beatles, C."

There, at the home of *Tonight's Unlikely Program*, Brother Zakarin begins.

"Now I want to make this easy for you," he says looking over my guideline or draft rundown as I refer to it, "But I also want to justify why the Hell I bought this thing."

One by one, Mark went down each name, each artist.

Who was *gettable*?

Which ones were Fred's, which ones were mine.

Whom can I go after to host these shows?

When is the delivery date?

What about clearing the rights to some of these scenes? How many songs per show?

There was a possible issue about the phrase, "screw you," in one of the scenes. We find out from Broadcast Standards that for a Nine or Ten o'clock show, "It's dicey but possible."

This is an actual statement coming from the same network that approved, "douche-bag?"

That was Steven Bochco, whole different deal.

All these things that were familiar to me, that I had some experience in, except this time, I'm the one who gets hung from the highest tree if it fails.

Wow.

32

The other thing we had to cover was getting every potential worker bee, Network Approved.

There's too much money involved for any arbitrary decisions. Everything is checked and balanced: In all media, worldwide, in all universes, in perpetuity, world without end, a-men.

At this point I am told, "I'll have Business Affairs start at Eight so he can do *his* job but I'll make sure he's prepared to settle at Eight Twenty-Five and let CAA know that."

I have never dealt with numbers this high.

It is also stated that, ". . . this is an On-Air deal, with usual creative supervision by ABC."

Talent delivery requirements were simple. Out of a total eleven artists, Fred and I were only required to fulfill seven. That means we basically had a whole half "show" worth of latitude.

The proverbial, "Kid in the candy store."

Pun intended.

So I looked straight into Mark Zakarin's eyes and tried to sell him something else.

"God, I wish you were better."
~ Fred de Cordova

I leave ABC and drive straight to CAA.

"Make the first pass of the budget at Nine Hundred Forty; that gives us something to go on. They'll think we're lying at Eight Twenty Five," my agent suggests.

"I can, however Fred is certain we can do this for Six Fifty—that makes us lying at Eight," I say with a wink.

"Over Nine, and make sure you write 'Fuck you' in big red letters on the cover."

"So you want *everyone* to hate me?"

"Everyone did, the moment the boy producer partnered with the Legend. Get used to it."

On many occasions Fred would say that once dollar one has changed hands that it is very difficult for a Network to turn back. Knowing this, I was more than willing to adjust my initial "get started" request of One Twenty Five to Fifty, "We'll do what you want Mark, just be prepared that we'll be knocking on your door that much sooner," I said initiating good faith.

What do you think I liked the most with this particular project? It's not what you might think.

It brought out the kid in everyone.

I was told this show had an *aura*. I don't know about that but there were many unusual and unlikely things about the deal, the show, and especially the talent interest.

Fred simply and affectionately called it, *The Big Show*.

Jack Lemmon told me that, "This will be the most fun I've had since the days of live television."

Not a bad endorsement.

Production crew who had thirty to forty years' experience in broadcast television felt that, "This is so different," or "I don't have to 'phone this in'," or some saw they had an opportunity to, "Break the rules a little bit."

Out of the blue, I received a phone call from John Ritter who stated, "You've restored my faith in network television. I'd like to figure something out with you so I can be a part of your party."

Many times I heard from representatives of certain artists, "How did you sell something like this?"

My joke usually was, "I said performance-driven instead of Variety."

Kevin Spacey's reps called.

Agents are usually re-active not pro-active.

A pleasant voice speaking the Queen's English calls to tell me, "They'll love this in England."

Refreshing change, I think.

The voice continues to tell me about a song that he is about to demo and begins to explain the entire back-story behind the lyrics. He then assures me that it has a rhythm & blues feel and—

No Musicals on this show!

"Hang on one moment and let me get my guitar." On that cue, the very distinctive voice of Elvis Costello entertained my office on the speakerphone.

It seemed that with every artist we had to go after, five new ones came back. We were flexible to accommodate and if a certain *multi-hyphenate* performer had difficulty deciding whether to act or perform music, we were more than pleased as producers to say, "Do both and we'll put one *in the bank*."

I was able to get CBS approved for the location where we were to shoot this thing and so I felt I had a best-of-all-worlds situation. For Fred, it was a symmetrical "coming home" of sorts.

One day, we were walking toward the elevators in what is called the "East Building" at historical CBS, when we were practically attacked by an older gentleman who looked as if he were a *lifer* at the studio.

"Mr. de Cordova! Mr. de Cordova!"

"Yes, darling."

"I was your Stage Manager on 'The George Goble Show', and—"

"Marvelous show that was—"

"And I felt so honored having the chance to work for you."

"Well, it was a pleasure working with you as well," Fred compliments.

"I mean, you haven't changed a bit. You look the same as you did in 1956."

"As do you," Fred peers at which floor the elevator could be on.

"So are ya doin' somethin' for us? Cause if ya are, I'd sure love the chance to work with you again."

The elevator opens and we step in.

"We'll have to look into that," Fred says, pressing the button repeatedly.

"I'll come to your office later and give you my card."

"Can't wait."

The elevator door closes.

Fred turns to me, "Who the fuck was he?"

We were treated so well at CBS. Steve Schifrin and his boss Charles "Cappy" Cappelman took care of our production office needs. And treated Fred like a king.

On Fred's "first day" I promised to give Steve a heads up call so that he and Cappy could welcome Fred face to face.

Fred walked in with a desk plate that read simply, *Mark Handles That*.

As we all sat in my office, Cappy recounted a time when he was a stage manager for The Jack Benny Program. At sixteen, he said he was in awe of this famous movie director turned television producer/director who ran to the foot of the stage at a moment when everything was in upheaval, raised both hands and shouted, "Stop! Nobody help me." Then one by one, he proceeded to fix everything.

Cappy concluded, "We may not have you on our network but we are honored to have you under our roof."

With that, he gave Fred a gift, courtesy of CBS.

Dennis Miller, whose offices were down the hall, indicated to me that our *Tonight's Unlikely Program*, sign made him laugh every morning he entered the elevators.

I told him that laugh was three forth's of the reason the show probably sold.

Feeling a little more confident, I tried to see if he wanted to participate but he was a little cautious at first regarding what he called his . . . *acting band.*

Above all, there was my friend, my partner in this so-called party, Fred de Cordova. He was the biggest kid of all.

I remember bumping into a couple Tonight Show acquaintances in which the general consensus was what did I do to Fred, that he's walking on air and that he'll probably live another twenty years.

After comments like that I always had an itch to look over my shoulder.

Now one particular moment that stands out during these beginning stages of our show was the day we had what was dubbed a "Looks like and Sounds Like," creative meeting at the Network with Mark Zakarin.

Why does this stand out?

I had an opportunity to see a man in his eighties, come to our new temporary offices at CBS Television City that morning, head on over to ABC to talk about the show, come back to CBS for the re-cap and on to finish out the day at NBC to fulfill his consulting obligations with The Tonight Show.

When Fred stood in the parking lot, he looked at our two cars together, looked back at me and said, "When I go home tonight, I'll have been at all three Networks."

"That's as it should be," I said.

That was the moment that surpassed *any* deal.

"Turn up the heat."
~ Fred de Cordova

It is December in Los Angeles. Cold, rainy, flu season.

Add to that, the passing of two national treasures and Fred's dearest friends, Mr. Dean Martin and Mr. Gene Kelly.

So, I found it no coincidence that Fred fell ill and due to his age had to check into Cedar's. I was worried.

When I called, in typical fashion, he barked, "Never mind me, how's our fucking show?" And added, "Don't worry, I'm back in; beginning of next week. . . . And don't tell anybody."

And there you are.

As for the show itself, Talent was being coordinated, sets were being built, Directors being approached and decided upon, there were two alterations made regarding the delivery requirements but we were, "able to replace with someone of equal or greater value."

We had a February sweeps delivery. We were satisfied with our production dates so that in the nick of time: We'd be able to *cut and paste* the segments, followed by taping the host's *bridges*, the material would be *cleared for broadcast*, so that two weeks after said delivery, we would hopefully be enjoying it as we would also be incredibly drunk.

There were a few things, as we approached the upcoming New Year that seemed a little unsettling.

First, there was a "Mark Zakarin can't be disturbed," period for two weeks.

Second, a friend at CBS said he saw, "Your buddy [Mark] talking to [CBS VP] Billy Campbell," to which my immediate response was, "Jesus, they play basketball together for chrissakes. Stop being paranoid."

Then I realized that people pay me to be paranoid, so I started thinking.

So far, three hundred thousand dollars have been invested, five hundred remaining from the earmarked eight; the contract has not been signed yet and I am awaiting our red lined copy.

I call my contract attorney Les Abell.

"In Paragraph Nine, would you include this?"

(Paragraph Nine basically says, "If you don't deliver what we want, you owe us the money we gave you.")

"Make sure it says . . . and such inability (to deliver) is not attributable to any act or omission by ABC."

Les asked me, "That's pretty good, where did you go to school?"

"Barnes & Noble," I say, "And the Fred de Cordova school of *Just in Case.*"

I had no idea how that little line would serve us so well down the bumpy road of show business.

> ## "These fucking holidays are such a bore."
> ## ~ Fred de Cordova

One message blinks on my home answering machine.

"You and I have put together a truly remarkable *beginnings of a program*. I am happy particularly since many of these names are, on almost all occasions, totally unavailable for anything but what they do in their regular activities. You can combine people that are impossible to combine. I love you. We work well together. I hope this fucking holiday goes quickly. I want you to know that I will be dinnering and speaking fondly about you and The Big Show. I hope, as I am, that you are celebrating Jesus. By the way, 'Desert Hawk' is on channel 256. A fabulous movie that I think you might enjoy. Please turn it on now. Bye."

Click.

> ## "Taping the show is more important than anything."
> ## ~ Fred de Cordova

It is January the eighth, most people are back from break, our production dates are locked, we have a mid February delivery for a February sweeps air.

Fred sits across my desk, contemplating our cork board. This high-tech device is placed on an adjacent wall and has multi-colored three by five cards: Each Talent name and the status of each are indicated by the color of the card. Pink is locked, Blue indicates "almost there," White is "nothing has been done," and also some cards have red marker letters which state either "T" for travel, "H" for hotel, etc. The board serves also as a calendar to visually display what day said Talent is to perform and what the performance is going to be. This approach may be something left in antiquity but the damn method still works.

My assistant completely avoids the intercom and barks out each call.

"Arthur for Bob Newhart line one. Larry for Vince Gill line two. Stephen for Joni Mitchell with a quick question line three. Miller for Carrey returning and Mark Zakarin."

"Send Mark through, it's their football," I parrot the tone.

"We must be busy," deadpans a droll Fred.

ABC wanted us to fax a list of confirmed names as well as to coordinate a creative meeting within the next couple of weeks. Although I felt that we covered the creative bases at our "looks like and sounds like" meeting and frankly it seemed to both of us a little on the late side, we certainly were not going to initiate friction. I also heard ABC wants to air our show May sweeps, which I liked better.

I called my *Deep Throat* at CBS to see if there was any validity about what he had said before Christmas.

I heard that Mark Zakarin is not going to land at CBS.

Maybe it was just Hollywood gossip.

I phoned CAA to book this next so-called creative meeting at ABC.

It was agreed by and between Nightingale Productions, its representatives at CAA and ABC that the meeting take place January 18th, at 11:00 a.m.

Fred and I kept our collective eye on the ball.

His dinners and my hundred calls a day.

"Don't be afraid to be a jerk, this is show business."
~ Fred de Cordova

I usually am the first one to arrive at the office.

Fred would be a half hour after that.

This one morning, the phone rings and it was my agent.

"What's this I hear about Fred backing out of the show?" Accuses the Armani voice.

"What?" I react, not understanding.

Fred walks in.

Armani repeats, "I had heard an ugly rumor that your partner backed out of the show."

"Well aside from the fact that your source sucks, let me ask you one question. Who is the older guy sitting next to me smoking up my office right now?" I posture.

"I just didn't want you to embarrass yourself," drones the ten-percenter.

"Okay, Fred?" I ask, looking at him, "Are you backing out of our show? 'Cause I don't want to embarrass myself'," I direct my attention back to my protective agent, "There. I double checked. Just in case. Happy?"

"I'm sorry," he backpedals.

"Why didn't you stop the lie right then and there? You, who are supposedly on our team, perpetuated this merit-less gossip by being wishy-washy. Actually, you did it twice. Once from your shitty source and a second time even mentioning it to me. Next time I want to embarrass myself, I'll consult you."

"Any one who says that I am backing out of this show is a clear example of someone trying to cover their ass. You better not forget," Fred says with a grin, "I'm on your side."

And that never wavered.

"Vodka helps."
~ Fred de Cordova

We start shooting in one week and it is the morning of our meeting with ABC.

Lights are up, the floor is painted and now for the first time, what had been merely an idea from the ether, I watch as my sets are being delivered to Studio 36.

I cried.

It was as if our wonderfully talented designer, Roy Christopher, reached in my brain and plucked out what I saw (and was Network Approved).

All Fred could say was, "This is good."

My response? . . .

"Thank you."

Upstairs in our offices, we made some phone calls and waited for the car to pick us up.

Everything was as ready as it could have been. All our paperwork, organized. My representative at CAA was to meet with us at the Network, and it felt as if everyone was on the same page when that Armani voice calls me.

"We need to reschedule. I have a luncheon with George Lucas," says my timely agent.

Fred was a little annoyed as was I but then he made the suggestion for CAA to go ahead with their lunch and we would still honor the meeting with ABC and that perhaps our contract attorney, Leslie Abell, would make an appearance in their stead.

CAA reluctantly agreed.

Since there is never rest for the weary or maybe it's a Murphy's Law type situation but one of our key Top-Flight Talent Artists (Please note: Delivery Requirements) called with some *issues*.

This definitely required some Fred finesse but that meant he'd have to stay behind. He would always say, "Let the Network reschedule you not the other way around."

As a result, I brought one of our other producers for another set of ears and his expertise in production to come with me and Fred made sure I told ABC where he could be reached and that he, "Sends his best."

We all gathered in Mark Zakarin's office.

Small talk ensues when the door opens and Mark stands.

"John is going to be joining us," Mark states as John Hamlin enters with another gentleman I have never met face to face before from Business Affairs.

If you haven't spotted the mark in the first half-hour at the table, you're it.

"I thought this was a Creative meeting," I discretely whisper to my attorney Les, clearly indicating how *not* a good sign this is.

"I asked John to be here because I have already notified ABC that I will be leaving effective immediately and that John here will be your Creative lead on the show."

John? . . . The Fred's-most-tactless-moment . . . John?

"I'm honored you would want to participate in helping us see this through. Thank you," I say in an Academy Award winning performance.

I'm fucked, I'm fucked, I'm fucked and I'm fucked.

"Well, let me hand out our schedule and I guess I'll give this to just John then, okay?" I express to Mark with a "deer in the headlights" look on my face that I couldn't conceal.

"Sure, that's correct," Mr. Zakarin nods pretending not to notice.

I turn to Mr. Business Affairs who appears not to have liked me on sight, "Would you like this as well?"

"Yes, please."

John Hamlin rubs his forehead and from the first word he (re)mixes and (re)matches the performers that we'd spent time putting together, suggests getting rid of others, he doesn't want any scenes from plays but movies only; he changes the amount of music, the host and the title too. Now that may seem crazy and I must confess as it was happening, his approach didn't feel great but when one takes a step back to see where he is coming from, it can be a different story.

First, it is possible that Mark's leaving was a surprise to everyone. Also you figure that his departure has a significant effect on let's say, ten other shows just like ours.

Second, we could have been canned right then and there. This is not the case and John Hamlin, at the very least, likes some of what we've done so far and is willing to oversee this on top of his already existing award show franchise(s) that gear up this time of year.

Third, when this happens, the new Executive wants to put his thumbprint on it. He doesn't want to be stuck with the last guy's failure but also to some extent does not want the last guy's success either.

Fourth, this was not an awards show.

We now enter the blessing/curse phase.

John is not aware of any previous conversations or negotiations that I have already had from Mark other than the standard delivery requirements which have now changed because of his modifications that Fred and I will have to enforce in less than a week.

But it still is the Network's football.

"We will let you know no later than Friday what we have decided," John says as I stand up and thank each one of them.

How fun, now I get to tell all of my employees!

My second Academy Award winning performance occurred when I entered our offices.

"How'd the meeting go?" One employee asks.

"Just great," I say without missing a beat, "Where's Fred?"

While Fred and I are working out our battle plan we hear that ABC is considering canceling the show(s).

Then, the show is back on.

Finally, at five o'clock, Friday, I receive a call from John Hamlin which begins, "By noon Monday," and ends with every change John has made followed with the required written confirmation from all respective new and/or altered Talent signed off by their representatives.

"Then I guess we'll be speaking Monday afternoon, have a good weekend Mr. Hamlin, thanks."

> "I have two objectives with this show. One, to see this get on the air, and Two, to see you move ahead."
> ~ Fred de Cordova

Monday arrived and just after high noon, there is a conference call between me, Leslie Abell my attorney, John Hamlin and the gentleman from Business Affairs who has not mellowed since last Thursday.

"We are halting the production to re-tool," John Hamlin states matter-of-factly.

"Are you pulling the plug?" Les Abell inquiries pushing the envelope as far as it can go.

"No," then John continues, "Until such time that your client and I can agree on a new set of circumstances i.e. Talent, Director, Host, 'the elements,' no further monies will be released to further fund the production."

"What about hot costs, we prepared for the first day of tape which was scheduled in three days, Mr. Hamlin," I interject.

"We will have a meeting within ten days to discuss the show, see you then my boy."

Let the Baptism begin.

"This wasn't a fucking step deal, for chrissakes."
~ Fred de Cordova

Well we had quite a chess game on our hands and I'll bet the Network felt the same way. I am also conscious of the fact that in this type of situation, both "sides" are right and both "sides" are wrong.

Regardless, it is up to Fred and me to respond fairly, steadily and in good faith no matter what the appearance of the challenge that faces us.

ABC, to produce the first show has already invested three hundred thirty three thousand dollars. We have ten days to two weeks to regroup and construct a *new* show under John Hamlin's supervision. We have to notify all previously planned Talent as well as their representatives that the show has been halted. And I am going to have to get a lay of the land regarding our facilities at CBS to see if we can't find alternative dates for taping what basically amounts to a brand new "second" show. With typical steadfastness, CBS responds with, "No worries, we will always make room for you."

Clearly, there was new work to be done and Fred and I both have renewed determination to deliver John's shows and make him happy.

> "I can say with some certainty that John will want to deal with just you. I am not an asset but I will call if you feel it is necessary."
> ~ Fred de Cordova

Fred made it crystal clear that I need not worry about the Talent and that my main concern should be to focus on my relationship with John Hamlin.

John requests a Director of his own choice.

I ask Fred to call the Director first.

I am excited that this successful Director and I seem to get along, that he wants to meet and asks permission to speak with Hamlin regarding the show.

ABC requests the material we have thus far.

Scene and song synopses with a draft script are messengered.

There is a call from the Network.

"What do you expect me to do, read this shit?"

Click.

Guess I'm the horse and Hamlin knows how to ride.

My third call from the Network concludes that most scenes and actors are not approved but *we* are aware that it is not the Network's job to know what they're looking for but rather it is up to us to show them what we *think* they're looking for so that they can let us know.

If it were easy—

Back to the drawing board.

My first face to face meeting with the Emmy award-winning director went well. He comforted me (somewhat) by saying that John shows no discrimination with any producer and confided that he deals with the same thing himself.

My agent indicates that we'll need more money or we will be forced—by our own accord—to halt.

I gave him my assurances that we *had that covered*, that we were fine for now, and *not* to ask for the second third of the license fee but perhaps request just sixty thousand as an act of good faith due to my newly acquired relationship. My theory was that if they released anything, that alone would validate all our additional new work.

Business Affairs had no problem with that request.

John wanted to approve more material and will not release more money until he is satisfied that there is movement.

Fred takes a puff and tells me that we're doing fine, "...but don't you dare give up. We'll figure this out."

We submit additional material.

The ratio of "Approved" is greater than "Not Approved" in this third call from ABC Creative. We are making apparent headway and I for one am getting a better understanding of the "likes and dislikes."

"Thank you, Mr. Hamlin."

"We'll speak with you tomorrow, my boy."

I will not call him John until he says I can.

We submit a final round of new material, intended actors that could be packaged with that material, songs and their respective artists and capped it with a mock up sizzle reel.

The response was positive and there was enough for forty-four minutes of air time with a little protective overflow. In other words, we scored.

We still were asked to change the title because, "*Unlikely* is too negative."

"Not a problem, Mr. Hamlin, thank you."

"All right, my boy."

Business Affairs sends the first diatribe of many to my attorney. I am not presented in a very good light.

That notwithstanding, we now have a deadline of ten days to two weeks to get written confirmation from the new Talent, secure necessary rights for the new material and pray that we can squeeze in at CBS mid April for the ABC dictated May sweeps air.

One day just prior to our dead line date, my contract attorney receives a voice mail phone message from Mr. Business Affairs who in a hushed tone says, "Tick tock, tick tock, tick tock."

Click.

Fred de Cordova and I wait impatiently on the day of our deadline and as a result of our follow through, ABC Creative will not pull the plug but still will not release any portion of the remainder of the license fee.

Not a real confidence builder.

Fred wonders why we haven't received full Creative approval regarding our Network suggested Director.

Because they are changing they're minds.

Huh?!

I fight to keep this Director with us and then thought how odd this was.

"We either need to commit or exploit this elsewhere. Don't you think it's time to settle Fred?"

"I'd rather just get the damned thing done. I've never quite been treated like this before by a Network," indicates a puzzled mentor.

> "I . . . for me I would blow my top. If you had this discussion with Hamlin, he would then become your enemy. I strongly suggest you avoid this discussion at all costs. Put it in a letter and let me read it.
> God bless you, darling."
> ~ Fred de Cordova

We sent a "let's protect our investment and meet," letter to John.

No response, however another unpleasant Business Affairs letter followed peppered with typical hyperbole.

Meanwhile, Talent, their agents, publicists and/or managers continue to call and inquire or in some cases wonder what is going on.

One late night musical artist who expressed extraordinary interest in what we were up to, had his manager call and stated that his client would rather be a part of our show in some way and decline President Clinton's request to perform on the Kennedy Center Honors.

Why does that excite me and make me queasy at the same time?

Finally and always what seems at the right time, Fred has a call with John Hamlin.

John tells Fred that he thinks *I* can't clear any of the material he wants and that perhaps he should pull the plug.

"But I have all this paperwork that I wanted to present," I say to Fred feeling grateful he made the Godfather call.

"I know and I think you know what to do about that."

"He's not going to return my call with this belief of his."

"It is your job to protect the temporary livelihoods of others and if you have something that sheds light, go do it."

"Thanks Fred."

"I have faith in you."

I gathered my paperwork and took a little drive to the American Broadcasting Company. On the fifth floor, I gave a cordial hello to the receptionist and made my way down the hall passing John's assistant ending up in the doorway of his office.

"Boo," I said with folder in hand, "I have a mountain of information that I think will have some value to you and wanted to messenger it personally."

"I don't have any time," he says.

"I understand, just a drop off."

"Let me see it."

"Yes sir."

I hand him the folder and he takes a glance at its contents.

"You can have a seat while I look through this."

"Thank you, Mr. Hamlin."

Thirty minutes later, we make agreements, we settle and he will not pull the plug. He did make some suggestions on making some staff changes which made sense to me. He also told me that he felt that our show was too big for my agent and gave me some remedies to investigate. I obliged because the show is king or as Fred would often chant, "We're all replaceable."

"Thank you for stopping by," said a grinning John.

"Hey, thank you sir," I said as I stood up to shake his hand.

I practically ran to the lobby, called Fred to tell him it was good, that I would go into detail later but I had to call Les Abell.

"Get off the fucking phone and call him."

"You're what?" Said an amused contract attorney, "You're where?" And, "How on God's Earth did you manage a meeting with Hamlin?"

"We have a deal as you know."

ABC Business Affairs phones Les Abell.

"I have to take this, it's our friend."

And with just a touch of admiration, Mr. Business Affairs states, completely avoiding salutation, "I saw your guy in the lobby talking on the phone. What's he doing here?"

Fanning his feathers, Les declares, "As you know, we have a deal at ABC and my client was just finalizing certain aspects with John for the last half hour."

A stifled chuckle from ABC and then, "Hamlin likes your guy, Bennett. He's got guts. No one does what Mark Bennett is doing with John Hamlin. So what are the terms."

Back at the office, Fred tells me, "People are still working because of what you did."

"What *we* did."

"I beg to differ."

I try to explain that there's no way in the world I could do any of this without his constant help.

"The show has legs because of you."

"It is our unlikely partnership that gives it legs. I mean it's like L.B. Mayer and Irving Thalberg," I say with the biggest wink.

"Yes, and I knew them both."

We sat there, quiet for the longest time.

"I must say," Fred breaks the silence as he takes out another NOW cigarette, "I never had a son, but if I did I would want him to be you."

I had no response.

> "Just when you think you don't have the show is when you have the show. The converse is also true."
> ~ Fred de Cordova

Our star Director has recommended that we hold off on our tape days because . . . "We have a real jewel on our hands, let's not rush into things and start from scratch."

ABC Business Affairs sends a memo validating everything that was previously discussed by John and me.

What was to come and what we didn't know?

Two twenty year veterans of ABC were to change capacity and move on to greener pastures in mere weeks: President Ted Harbert and John Hamlin.

This would enable the Network to walk away from our deal.

Fred de Cordova had something else in mind.

On August 5th, 1996, Fred wrote to our Business Affairs' superior, Sr. Vice President, Mr. Mark Pedowitz. He wrote:

Dear Mr. Pedowitz,

I have not had the pleasure of speaking with you but felt the need to express my personal and professional experiences I have had with Mark Bennett on paper, specifically my knowledge and input regarding *Tonight's Unlikely Program*, a Special initially ordered by Mark Zakarin and then subsequently handed over to John Hamlin to be aired on ABC.

I have been a part of this project since its inception and have been pleasantly surprised at the excitement Mark Bennett has generated, as well as his ability to sell, coordinate and lock in such diversified top-flight talent in what, in my opinion, is a more original idea than I have seen cross my desk in many, many years.

I have participated in two meetings at ABC Entertainment personally with Mr. Bennett. I am aware of the eleven artists stated in the original agreement under Zakarin.

Mr. Bennett confirmed seven and the eighth "yes" occurred after Mark Zakarin's departure.

Mark Bennett is flexible and he approaches the unplanned with consistent good humor so I knew while the adjustment to my friend, John Hamlin, would be difficult as with any sudden changes within the corporate family, Mr. Bennett would quickly establish a good working relationship so as not to hamper the progress of the show. I feel that because of John, Mark delivered an even better show than what was originally intended.

My only concern was while Mark was re-tooling with John, that Nightingale Productions would be compensated for the obvious push costs incurred by ABC's postponing of the first tape day on January 22nd. I told Mark to let CAA know that.

Subsequently, while John was in Monaco, I was surprised again when Mr. Bennett went ahead and personally cleared all the material himself, approved by John as well as going back to "dead" material and turning certain "no's" into "yes's." I recall specifically "Tootsie" which Mark jokingly referred to as a Hamlin favorite.

I am aware of companies that have a change of heart regarding certain projects. I know if ABC was to re-address *Tonight's Unlikely Program*, they would find its creator, Mark Bennett, just as enthusiastic, tenacious, fast; and with no ill will, able to deliver something we both have felt all along would and will be truly "a special."

I am confident there is no one other than Mark who could pull this event off with such class and aplomb.

Sincerely,

Fred de Cordova

And he carbon copied eleven additional individuals. *Yikes.*

> "I need to think about this because if I call her
> right away, I'll say her perception of this
> thing is all fucked up."
> ~ Fred de Cordova

"For many years, I have admired your career," reads the immediate response from Mr. Pedowitz, "The matter referred to in your letter to me dated August 5, 1996 is being handled by the Business Affairs and Legal Staff. The facts as they have been explained to me differ from those outlined by you. We wish to thank you for your concern in this matter."

Reading this response, my first thought was: Letter? What letter?

A member of our staff said simply, "Fred's letter is a choir."

No kidding!

Well, if there was any shot at all to get this thing out of *Turnaround*, this was definitely it. I recognized that *my* ability, or alleged inability, was being challenged, and there was no one left on the Creative side to come to my aid. All I knew (Fred notwithstanding) is that I had worked too hard and spent too much money sandwiching myself around wiser, more experienced people who were completely capable to deliver this show, to *not* take another turn at bat.

I really didn't care if there was a *fly in the ointment* on the Corporate side, but I told Fred that if I am going to be the scapegoat, that I should go alone on this one and that it might show Mr. Pedowitz that I can take my licks.

Fred agreed and added, "I'll know the result when you ask me to call this new gal whom I'll just refer to as Executive Number Three."

Jitters aside, I placed the call to the office of Mark Pedowitz. I was ready for anything (including, "Don't call this office ever again."). I had every document to show our dots connected Talent wise, the papers that indicate fiscal responsibility, I had the results from the clearance company we had hired, hell I even included pictures of all our beautiful sets. Now all I needed was an okay to meet.

"Mr. Bennett, it's your meeting."

So began a forty minute make or break meeting between Mr. Mark Pedowitz and me, the essence of which was to ask permission of him to take our show back to Creative and complete it.

"Go ahead and we will not impede or block the creative progress of the show."

I stood up, gratefully thanked him and shook his hand knowing with certainty that Fred's letter was the sole reason I was there in the first place.

Now it is up to us to work it out with this new individual, Executive Number Three.

Our car, this time, is driving over Coldwater Canyon.

"Now, if I show you where Robert Evans lives can we turn this thing around and go back home?"

"It's your fault we're doing this. You had to write that *Don't fuck with my son* letter," I say.

"I guess this means we're not in trouble anymore," and with an exaggerated gesture using both hands Fred announces, "HE LIVES RIGHT THERE."

"Thanks Fred. Could we still swing by ABC?"

"I suppose. What I'd like to know is just exactly how many executives are we going to have to go through to get this thing on the air? I was pretty certain that you only needed one *yes*."

"You've been wrong all these years."

"Let's see if I've got this straight so far," Fred begins as if this requires the utmost concentration, "For this particular project: We have garnered two *yes's* from Creative, one *yes* from Business Affairs and Legal, only to go back to Creative again to receive what I am assuming to be, a third *yes*. Is that right?"

"Yes."

"That makes five."

Fred executes another George Burns smoke take then asks, "Do you know this gal we're meeting now?"

"No. I know her background though."

"Fuck her background. I just hope she's not a cunt."

I told Fred that we had spoken twice, that I was afraid she may not like inheritance, but why worry since she may be gone in a couple weeks.

Fred pauses to smoke another, "Do you think that the new President is at all aware of what has transpired?"

"I don't know," I say pondering his statement.

"Set something up with President Tarses."

"Won't we piss somebody off?"

"If we word this correctly, it is nothing more than a thank you meeting for how generous ABC has been with us. Besides it would be good for the two of you to meet."

"Even though we are talking with Number Three now?" I ask, feeling this is all downside.

"It is exactly because we're talking to Number Three that we need to also welcome and thank this new President whom I feel has a similar road to travel as do you. Besides, if 'Three' gets fucked, hopefully we won't get included."

"Let's just see what happens today before I start bugging Jamie Tarses."

"That's fine," Fred states with a grin.

"This meeting's gonna go well, I've got that feeling in my gut," declares the boy producer.

"I have a Doctor for that," says the Legend.

"I hope I didn't say too much but I just had to make my points."
~ Fred de Cordova

"Can I get you anything Mr. de Cordova?" Asks our Third Entertainment Executive.

"Vodka but Mr. Bennett here will help me with that later. I'm fine for now."

We sit. We pitch. Out comes the paperwork.

Did she just say, "Of course it's doable?"

"It is truly the most original idea I've seen cross my desk . . ."

"Here are some potential Talent names . . ."

I heard it, she just said getable!

"Mark, show her the agreements and the favored nations arrangements you made for the scenes and songs . . ."

Wait, she just said, "Let's finish this thing."

"I just want to say this one thing."

Fred, did you hear that? She just said that we wouldn't have received the license fee if it were not produceable.

"Never in my twenty five years of booking Talent have I..."

She said okay!

Fred kept selling. I listened and realized how much I loved him and that even the best teachers can fall back on old taboos.

On Saturday, an excited contract attorney tells me that Executive Number Three ". . . is ready for someone (my agent) to call and do the deal with Business Affairs."

We felt this was good news and conferenced to my agent and left word at his home.

Monday arrives.

Fred suggests a mid-February shoot because, "The earlier, the better for the Talent."

CBS confirms studio availability.

My agent is cautiously confident.

Much to my surprise Mr. Business Affairs states, "We're creatively on track."

Fred is thrilled and wisely suggests, "Don't answer the phone."

By Tuesday at five o'clock in the afternoon, a cavalier Executive Number Three with a sing-song voice leaves the message, "Try as I may, but I couldn't get a full Creative sign off on the show."

"Full Creative sign off? There's no one left!" Fred says searching for some humor.

"If she could get the sign off, she'd be a wonderful person," I reach back to days of yore.

"Fuck her. I was right. She's a cunt."

So, I picked up the phone and called Jamie Tarses, then the youngest and first *ever* woman President of any Network, let alone the American Broadcasting Company.

She agreed to meet face to face and was now aware of our money and more importantly, their money that had been invested not to mention our time.

As for Executive Number Three? She was on the way out.

A month and a half later, just six days before we were to have our meeting (and Fred always had a habit of this kind of serendipity), I received an excited phone call.

"I have just had a lovely time with The Marvin Davis' celebrating their daughter's marriage."

"That's great, Fred. I like being up-to-date on your social calendar."

"Smart ass, the reason I called is that I ran into a friend of ours."

"Not hard to do at a Marvin Davis party."

"It was the lovely Jamie Tarses," he flaunts knowing the whole time he'd top me.

I always loved that.

"I hope you realize, this get together coming up is happening because you chose to avoid Talent names and talk only dollars and cents. I told her that she will see that *the show,* and you, are worthy."

> "Try your best not to pay attention to things
> that are said about you: Unless it's good."
> ~ Fred de Cordova

I had yet to meet Jamie Tarses and I was already quite a fan. She was everything that can make Hollywood very skittish: Very young, powerful, she was a she, looked like she should be in front of the camera and was fearless enough to go nose to nose with anyone. Trailblazing firsts never have it easy and it doesn't help when journalists join in on the spin.

I don't think she was treated fairly at all but the main thing I recognized is that she was chosen to sit in that chair *for-a-reason* and that is an accomplishment in and of itself.

Two days before we were to go back to ABC, I had a lesson from Fred about only paying attention to the good stuff, but it came by way of gossip.

A friend said he had heard an ugly rumor about me. This was not unusual, backside chit-chat has happened to everybody and it has happened at various times in my life as well. But THIS one got under my skin because it involved the person we were about to meet. I thought, "God, not now."

The word on the street and the timing of it bothered me enough that I stormed into Fred's office and confessed, "Goddammit Fred, all these fucking people out there are going around and saying that the only reason that we have a deal at ABC is because I'm fucking Jamie Tarses."

Fred exhales smoke and quietly responds, "Good, you're fucking Presidents."

Thus endeth the lesson.

"If this *doesn't* work, I might have to ask you to sleep with her."
~ Fred de Cordova

"Hey, isn't that the house where Bugsy Siegel was shot?" I ask, surprised I hadn't noticed it before.

"Yes it is. But never ever refer to him as Bugsy. He hated that."

We're on our way to meet Jamie Tarses at ABC.

"Incidentally," Fred looks to me, "Greg Kinnear is leaving his show to pursue movies. You might want to look into that."

"Talk-show host?"

"Yes. I think you'd be quite good."

"Well," I say, "First we should turn around right now. The second thing that comes to mind is: Who could we approach to produce a late-night talk show? No one comes to mind. I'm sure you must know someone."

"That's very funny."

We're making our descent into Century City not long after Fred has taken a moment to point out where Billy Wilder resides.

"He has a sign, you know, above the door of his office which reads, 'What would Lubitsch do?'."

"Well I better start on mine that says, 'What would de Cordova do?'."

"Then you're sure to fuck up."

> "It is always important to keep a particular project or show *within the ranks* unless you are in the fucking situation that we're in now."
> ~ Fred de Cordova

We sit in the lobby of ABC Entertainment.

"I'm really glad we're here fifteen minutes early so that we can start this meeting twenty minutes late," Fred says with an eye-roll.

We are spotted by a passerby who shouts Fred's name.

Here we go again.

We stand.

This person had to say a quick hello and tell us about their first job in Hollywood which was in Correspondence on *The Johnny Carson Show*. It was a sweet encounter until this person started to pitch us the show that I believe was intended for someone at ABC.

When we sat back down, I asked Fred what he thought of that show idea and he responded, "Everyone has a right to pitch what they are passionate about and it is not up to us to determine whether it is sellable or not."

"My God, if it isn't Freddie de Cordova."

We stand in acknowledgement once again.

A star, television Producer and former ABC Executive, a legend, I've only seen in pictures, approaches.

Hugs, laughter and memories are exchanged when Fred takes a moment to introduce me as his employer.

Cue the laugh track please!

The Producer goes on his way and we sit back down.

I glance over at Fred and tell him, "I can't take you anywhere."

"We're moving around so much I feel as if I've done a round of golf."

Then, without warning, coming from around the corner, the President of the Network appeared. Jamie Tarses came out to greet us as well as escort us back to her corner office.

"I already like her," Fred whispered to me.

That million dollar feeling started to creep back as I watched Jamie, in front of us, nod and say hello to everyone who looked up. We were bathed in a corporate klieg light.

If it is true that one can tell how the meeting is going to go by the first few minutes—So far, so good.

We took our places at the coffee table: Fred on the couch and sitting across each other, Jamie and me.

"What have we got?" Jamie asks, moving the poinsettia center piece off to the side and looking directly at me.

Although we had been through quite a bit, we were able to remain fairly neutral, get our point across and spotlight the many pluses we had acquired. Fred pointed out that because of John Hamlin's Director recommendation, we were considerably fortunate ". . . as he says, *no* to most projects every day."

We all had a mutual understanding of why the show was purchased in the first place, why we were able to bend with different Executive's requirements, why the show is/was cost efficient, why it had a build-it-and-they-will-come aura with Talent and why the goddamn thing just wouldn't roll over and die.

As we laid every card on the table, I noticed a significant turning point. Something that had not been the case when I started out with Fred. I was no longer the kid in the room and we happen to be pitching someone that I could have taken to the Prom. This was a first, and for me it would be different from here on out.

We continued to nurture our *greenhouse* with other projects, as we always did: taking pitches from other writers, trying our best to package various elements and placing them at what we felt were the appropriate organization(s). But nothing garnered more excitement than our *Big Show*.

Our meeting with Jamie ended with a hug, a kiss on the cheek and, "Perfect timing, I'll be seeing so-and-so at six tonight—He'd be a perfect Creative lead to guide you."

I followed up with the "on paper overview" submission per Jamie to illicit a face to face with this new guy.

The decision from him was unceremoniously, "a pass."

"He must not be aware that he already bought it," Fred said with an ironic chuckle, "We'll have to re-address this at a later time."

And then I saw a sadness I had never seen before. For the first time, the student consoled the teacher.

The office seemed unnaturally quiet.

"What else we got," I said in an effort to distract.

There was one response.

"Damn."
~ Fred de Cordova

After brief reflection one might wonder what this show was all about. What was it that got all those people jumping? What on Earth came out of the ether and paid some people?

It was simple. . . .

Here's the original pitch:

A performance-driven show where unlikely artists perform scenes from plays as well as *unplugged* musical numbers all taking place *live* in an upscale restaurant/bar overlooking Manhattan's East River. (The bar idea came later from the Network in order to avoid it looking too *PBS*.)

An opportunity for Top-Flight Entertainers to, "do something they wouldn't normally do with someone contrary to their public persona."

Tonight's Unlikely Program: A one hour series for audiences of all ages.

When this was first pitched, the most recent example that we could point to was an incredibly memorable and replenishable Christmas Season duet sung by Bing Crosby and David Bowie. That was in 1970. Today, one has to look no further than the last awards show or singing contest.

The one thing that still makes this distinctive, after all this time, is that we felt that it was a contemporary spin on an old Variety tradition. *Midnight Special, Playhouse 90* and *Your Show of Shows*, morphed.

Our solution to eliminate the perceived *booking intensive* issue was to, "Shoot it like a movie and book it like *The Tonight Show*." In other words, each artist pair is taped separately and therefore *banked*. It is simply a *cut and paste* job. Once you have sewn together all your scenes and songs and created a central thematic through-line, you bring in the (Network Approved) host to provide *bridges* in order to help move the *story* along.

It was cost efficient in that like an awards show, all Talent was paid on a most favored nations basis. In this case all Talent would be paid seventy five hundred dollars.

Lastly, it was replenishable in that like a clip show, we would have the ability to repackage and resell segments to other markets.

All of that just because I asked the question: If I were President of the Network, what would I want to see?

> "In reviewing a project, always ask yourself, 'Why is this different?' If you can answer that, sell it so that you can spend the next few months turning it into something derivative."
> ~ Fred de Cordova

"Did you read the trades? I can't believe he didn't cancel. Did he cancel? Did you check all your messages?" Fred probes like a kid at Christmas.

We are on our way to pitch Les Moonves at CBS. On this particular morning, it was announced that aside from being President of the Network, he will also oversee CBS Inc., as well as Eyemark . . . suffice to say, he had girth.

Fred had not been feeling well and regardless of the magnitude of this event, I was more than willing to try and reschedule but I don't think anything would stop Fred from an opportunity to sell something. Besides, you want Mr. Moonves to reschedule you, not the other way around.

"By the way, I'm selling my membership at the Bel Air Country Club. I don't like golfing so early anymore. It's three hundred thousand dollars."

"Thanks Fred but I don't golf."

The car pulls up to CBS Television City.

As we get out, Fred starts a coughing fit so intense he loses his balance. I grabbed his arm.

"Are you okay, Fred?"

"I'm fine," he lies.

Fred literally shakes off the feeling and we enter the lobby.

"Sir, you'll need clearance," urges the guard.

"Fuck you," and Fred walks through the door.

"We're meeting Les," I placate.

As we make our way toward the elevators, a board meeting lets out. They recognize Fred.

"Keep walking. Don't stop," Fred whispers to me.

We enter the renovated third floor executive lobby.

Fred continues, "I think I'm a little nervous. My mouth is dry."

"I'm comforted by that."

Fred needles some more, "What are we selling? You know you didn't brief me on this. I'm going in cold. I hope you're prepared, you know he's a very powerful man."

"Mr. Moonves is ready to see you," announces an assistant who leads us to his office.

Fred walks ahead of me as I see over his shoulder, Les Moonves, The Godfather of Show Business.

"Mr. de Cordova, what a pleasure to see you."

"The last time I was in this office, it was *my* office."

"My God, when was that?" Les asks, playing along but seeking not to be outdone.

"Well, that was back in the Benny days. Burns and Allen, Jim Aubrey—"

"Who was President then?" Les spots the target.

"Hubbell Robinson was President," Fred willingly opens the door.

"I don't even *remember* Hubbell Robinson." And that's how it started.

They passed, but it was quite an honor for me.

> "Never completely discard anything because
> nothing ever is completely dead."
> ~ Fred de Cordova

Although probably true, this philosophy makes me twitch.

"I was looking in my diary and it was a year ago tomorrow that—" so began Fred's acknowledgement of an anniversary of sorts where he reminisced our meeting with Jamie Tarses and all the yes's and no's we had acquired for a very expensive nifty idea.

"I've been paying close attention," Fred continues, "To a very innovative gentleman over at ABC. I think he is someone you could talk to about *The Big Show*."

Oh God.

"It won't hurt to ask. Tastes change."

The gentleman in question is named Michael Davies who certainly had his own experiences in beating one's head against the wall to try and get a show on the air.

Although it may have felt that he was the only one who was passionate about his idea, he hung in there, yelled loud enough and finally ended up executive producing a little known show ABC had little faith in entitled *Who Wants to be a Millionaire*.

So, I guess one never knows and Fred knows how to recycle.

I still had reservations. I guess you could say that regarding *this* show I was kind of *over it*. The last time I even spoke of what we went through was a chance encounter with an older man who was very interested as to why we never received any *Kill Money* to make us go away. Turned out he was a head Business Affairs guy at Disney. Where was he during all that nonsense?

With a wince I made the call and strangely, I had an encouraging conversation with this Michael Davies and was pleasantly surprised that he wanted to meet with us.

I booked the meeting.

"I knew it," shouts an excited and eager Fred.

One hour later, I received word from Mr. Davies that he is "not allowed to meet with me regarding this project but definitely open to anything else we may have."

I was not surprised and in some ways, relieved.

Fred, on the other hand, is a Producer's Producer. He is always willing to "make one more call against all appearances." I suppose that is why people admire and respect him so much. Most people throw their hands in the air too soon (*Too soon?*). That is the huge difference between success and continued success. I also believe Fred had a score to settle, and this was his version of the last spray into the jungle before you hit the dirt.

Fred calls Mr. Business Affairs.

"My associate," Fred begins, "Mr. Mark Bennett settled with Michael Davies regarding a meeting about a show I've been involved with. Is it true, as I understand it that Business Affairs disapproved of such a meeting? I know that each time we've been to the Network, Entertainment approved."

Mr. Business Affairs responds by saying, "Mark says that money is owed on something he never delivered, could not deliver and did not have the ability to deliver."

Fred calmly responds, "There were meetings in which the requirements were brought."

"I had heard, he was trying to get around us by going to Disney."

"Mark is more patient than me."

Mr. Business Affairs forges ahead, "To the best of my knowledge, on that basis, it eliminates all issues concerned regarding owed money. He was unable to deliver the Talent—"

Fred interrupts, "I believe or it has *been* my belief that you can count on me with the Talent. It would not be impossible or frankly difficult in all my years booking. Not speaking for Mark but I think that is why he had faith in me."

There was no retort.

So Fred continues, "Just suppose I say, 'I can deliver the show.' I don't want to get into history. I'd rather just continue. I've been booking Talent for twenty-five years. Jack Lemmon is a friend of mine, Bob De Niro is a friend of mine but I would not approach them unless I knew there were certain assurances made by the Network. Now you tried to drive Nightingale into the ground financially and it didn't work. The Talent angle is silly. Now why can't we," Fred exaggerates a drag from his cigarette, "Suppose we consider this a brand new idea—"

"I have no—"

"With a guarantee," Fred pauses.

"I have no objection."

"That, requires something from you," and without waiting Fred continues, "A letter to Mr. Davies with language indicating that ABC doesn't owe any money and that this is a new submission by ABC."

"On that basis, I see no reason *not* to have the meeting."

"Mr. Bennett is not saying this, I am."

"It's on that basis, Fred."

"Mr. Bennett is not presenting a show, I am. I can deliver the Talent."

Mr. Business Affairs in an attempt to conclude, "You're a legend Fred, I could not *not* take your call. I have such respect for you."

Fred adds, "I don't want to wait a day or two. Mr. Bennett's idea and format are doable."

"All history is withdrawn on that basis."

Click.

> "You certainly want your money to outlive you but never ever outlive your money."
> ~ Fred de Cordova

"Excuse me ma'am, I'm looking for Fred de Cordova's room."

Before the nurse had a chance to answer, I heard a distant voice barking orders from down the hall.

"Never mind."

I walked down the hall feeling relief with every swearword uttered because it was a hope that he was just fine.

"Looks like you have a visitor," the nurse says as she discreetly makes her exit.

"Mark," Fred stretches his arms out, "I am so happy to see you. You look just great. I am not, I took a fall."

"Well, don't next time."

"Stupid, I just lost my balance."

"You're gonna be alright. You've said 'fuck' twice already."

"We have a meeting you know, at NBC in a couple weeks. I spoke to a friend of ours."

"Hey, if you want to give yourself time to—"

"No. I'll be fine. Here, look at this."

Fred turns up the sound, and I realized it was *The Burns and Allen Show*.

"Here we are at Cedars on George Burns Boulevard watching *The Burns and Allen Show*," Fred says with a big grin, "Now sit down and you just might learn something."

I held the hand of the show's Producer/Director as he pointed out all those things that only he would know.

"You are truly my dear friend."
~ Fred de Cordova

"You might want to get your hair cut on the way over," Fred says to me the morning of a pitch at NBC, "You look like Jim Morrison, were he a lawyer."

That is how my day began.

I met up with Fred at his office-for-life at NBC when he presented me with a folder and told me that he thought maybe I could use it someday if I had to.

In it was a "To Whom It May Concern" letter, the lyricism combined with the magnitude of its author would no more get me a job in Hollywood than someone who just arrived by bus. Ah, show biz.

I was moved by his written sentiment and as I looked up, Fred tells me, "Now when you meet this gentleman; Please introduce me. I'd like to meet him."

We prepped for our pitch and drove across the street to his parking space in what is called, "The Midway."

Like many times before, we walked down the halls of the National Broadcasting Company.

This time, Fred was really having difficulty. His breathing was heavy, and every step was slower than the one before.

It was the first time I saw the ageless Fred de Cordova—old.

"My legs just can't carry me like they used to."

I tell him we can stop for a minute.

"Christ no. Keep walking. Don't stop."

We arrive at the office of Rick Ludwin and I am grateful there is a ten minute wait.

"We have sure done well for ourselves. I have been to more fucking Networks in the last eight years than I have in the last twenty-five. We've been kissed and fucked many times over. Isn't it funny we're back where we started," says Fred, bemused.

We sat on this little couch in the bullpen that was probably purchased when *Laugh-In* was on the air. I had difficulty getting up and even though Fred normally wouldn't ask for help, he appreciated Rick's offer of a hand. Both Rick and I pretended nothing was unusual.

Fred led the pitch because he wanted to and damn if he still couldn't fill a room and captivate.

I knew what the result was going to be and so did Fred, I think, but that really wasn't the point.

I will always remember that day with bittersweet fondness as it would be the exact moment when my relationship with Fred forever changed.

> "I had dinner with Robert Evans last night,
> and we toasted our strokes."
> ~ Fred de Cordova

I remember finding out over the phone.

"Mr. De, can't take any calls right now," I hear a voice in the background and then Fred re-answers, "Hello Mark?"

"Jesus Christ, I leave you alone for a couple weeks and you go get yourself a stroke. What the fuck is up with that?" I act.

"Yeah, why weren't you there to stop it."

I did most of the talking, and we finished with I love you's and Fred asking, "Promise you'll keep calling."

"Always."

Two and a half months later and defying logic once again: Fred sits behind his desk, defiantly smoking, elegant as usual, the only difference is his speech—which is a little slower yet somehow works well for him.

We're laughing when Fred decides to "shift gears."

"Because of you, the last several years for me have been a real highlight—doing business," he says as I try to memorize every inch of his face, "You have proven yourself enough to show me that there is no reason for you not to be a big-shot in this industry."

I told him that I wouldn't mind doing everything all over again.

After a quick glance around the office, I notice a black three-ring binder filled with a veritable who's-who of show business. A stack of faxes all wishing a Happy Eighty-Ninth to a universally beloved Freddie.

"I didn't get this on *my* birthday," I joke.

"You will, when you're eighty-nine. Although it won't be any of those people, they'll all be dead."

Then, placed neatly in a side pocket were two cards I recognized.

I recall signing them, "Your smart-ass son."

Periodically, over the next four months, it seemed as if Fred would not rest until he felt I was professionally on a track that made sense to him. *The Big Show*, to Fred, was certainly a conversation starter. If that could be left in good hands as well as me it would be the best of all worlds.

Frequently, phone conversations from Fred to me would begin with things like: "I spoke with Barry Diller and . . . ," or "Don Mischer is truly a decent man and I think we . . . ," or "I've known Dick Clark for years, perhaps I can . . ."

After all these years, you'd think I would stop being surprised. Not so.

Conversations ensued, and that led to more conversations that at the very least appeared, at that time, to have benefitted me.

On Thursday, June 15th, 2000, I hear that my teacher had a second stroke. I drop everything to go see him at Cedars Sinai Hospital.

There is something very wrong about a man who has spent his life in communications having difficulty talking. Although that is consistent with Fred's humor.

"Standing right there," he sells as a nurse pours a solution in his water to make it thicker, "Standing there, is one of the most brilliant producers with whom I have ever worked."

That, bit of propaganda, was his response to a nurse asking if I was family.

"Close enough," I said.

We watched *The Rosie O'Donnell Show* and named the publicist or agent of each of her guest panelists.

He finally told me—at the commercial break—he was leaving a George Christy dinner. Don Rickles was there being, "very rude, but funny," and "Merv was there," and he added with effort, "I left, came home, turned on my television set and woke up like this."

With gestures and a shake of his head, he indicated that he couldn't hear out of one ear, couldn't see out of one eye and that he must have hit something as he was missing some teeth.

But he still could muster quite eloquently, ". . . and . . . I . . . can't . . . fucking . . . talk."

I laughed with a tear as I kissed him on the cheek.

A nurse came in to check on Fred. She had this sing-song voice that was very irritating when she asked how, "Mr. de Cordova is doing today?"

Fred rolled his eyes and yelled at me with just a glance.

I smiled.

The nurse told Fred that a doctor would be in shortly for examination, but he needed to be propped up in a better position, and she needed to step out to get some help.

I decided to make a brief exit to give Fred a little respectful privacy.

Over my shoulder, I hear a very comforting and familiar bark.

"No! He'll do it."

I turn around to see him pointing at me.

Leave it to Fucking Fred to throw me into uncharted waters.

I stood on one side, and Fred had hold of my wrist.

The nurse coached me as to where to hold the towel Fred was laying on.

I am cradling the man with that engulfing handshake.

And with a one, two, three—together, we propped him up. Fred mouthed the words, thank you.

A permanent memory.

> "I seem to recall a 310 area code, and
> you were doing quite well."
> ~ Fred de Cordova

I had to downsize. After my experiences with Fred, just trying to get a regular job became quite a challenge. One can almost feel unemployable until such time as one can re-invent one's self. I kept hearing I was over-qualified yet always thinking that I wasn't too over-qualified to eat.

This was an unpleasant period to go through, many challenges—professional transitions—and unfortunately I knew there were no short cuts. Of course, I could always fall back on my acting. . . .

Nightingale Productions was shuttered and I had no idea how to put that on a resume for someone in Human Resources.

God knows how to describe what my skills were, all I knew was that I couldn't type.

Having now entered the *famine segment* of the beginning producer's see-saw, I was amused that I had to draw up a document for Fred verifying his employment, and run it up to his house—from the Valley I might add.

Irony in this case did not sell me.

Yet Fred needed me.

The only issue was whether I had enough gas in my Jaguar XJ6 to get up to Trousdale Estates.

When I entered his home, he was seated in his office wearing a plush bathrobe.

I gave him the letter to approve the language, he nodded and I signed it.

It felt like old times.

> ## "Don't show this to me, give it to somebody who can fucking buy it."
> ~ Fred de Cordova

I am seated in his master bedroom.

I had handed a script to him, a one-hour comedy drama entitled, "Balancing Act," to be pitched at ABC.

As he held it in his hand as if to gauge its weight he said, "This feels about nine hundred fifty thousand."

"I'll submit your name as an Executive Consultant," I said.

"Then it will be a well consulted show."

"You bet, Fred."

Fred continues to eat his pureed lunch and takes a sip of his O'Doul's. He is a month into his ninetieth year.

"Are you making a living?"

"Modest. People keep returning my calls. Yes."

"Good, you should be."

"Fred, I truly believe, the only reason I can walk in the front doors of ABC is because of you. Kind of like both sides won and both sides lost."

"That man," Fred shakes his head and waves both hands, "Is no longer there."

I smile because Fred's "bite" is as strong as ever.

"Well, whatever the reason, wish me luck," I get up to give him a hug adding, "One thing is certain, it sure isn't as fun doing this alone as it is doing it with you."

"Never is."

I laugh knowing he was referring to something else.

Fred smiles, "You'll be just fine."

I also knew he meant something more than the meeting at hand.

"By the way, I saw a bunch of Tonight Show guys, and they wanted me to make sure to tell you that they think of you, they miss you, and they send their best."

"Tell them, I don't miss them."

"Mark Bennett speaking fondly about me?
Tell him to stop."
~ Fred de Cordova

"When do I see you?" Asks *that* voice.

"Whenever you want," I say.

"Wednesday, one o'clock."

"That's my birthday, Fred."

"Really, I had no idea," he exclaims in mock surprise.

Well, some things never change.

On my birthday day, with no updates, no day's recaps, no budget passes or deal memos: I make my way through Coldwater Canyon just to hang out with my dear pal, Freddie.

"There's Mark," Fred sits upright atop a perfectly made King bed. He looks cozy, arms crossed.

A baseball game plays on the television. It's on mute.

"You are my birthday present," I say as his nurse enters.

Fred introduces me and explains all the work we had done and shared together.

I notice an oxygen tank tucked in the corner of the room.

"I just dated a nurse last week. We don't even have to talk, and I'm still picking up traits from my mentor."

Fred sizes me up, "You look just terrific. So handsome. Healthy."

"Thanks Fred," I say loudly over his coughs—and sit.

I study the room. Opposite Fred, there is a wall to wall bookcase: Eight Emmy's, Tiffany frames and books by the hundreds. *Is that a painted portrait of Angie Dickinson on that wall?*

"I don't think you realize how loved you are in this industry," he says slowly.

I didn't know how to respond as I was certain he was mistaken.

"And I want you to know that every good wish I could ever have, I give to you."

What's this feeling of finality? You'll get better.

"How old are you, young man?"

I told him.

"I was that age a long time ago."

And with that, Fred reminisced. Of Bud Robinson pool parties and all-night cards, of Irving Lazar Oscar parties and David O. Selznick word games. He spoke fondly about a birthday party for Cole Porter and laughed at the memory of a young and drunk Richard Burton, kissing everybody.

"You look tan. Doesn't he look great?" Fred asks his nurse and adds, "That man is a marvelous Producer. You just wait and see what's next."

"Hoping of course, a *next* will happen," I say.

"There was one show," Fred shares with this apparently always present RN, "How many Networks?"

"Most of them," I interject.

"Two paid us," Fred says and gestures with two middle fingers and adds, "Mark kept it going," he coughs, then points to himself, "And kept me working after that."

"We've got some great sets if you'd like them," I tell the nurse.

"I've been thinking," Fred addresses only me, "We've got this writer's strike, and it might be interesting since *The Big Show* was entirely scenes and songs already published, you could shoot the whole show or many shows, never having to need a writer."

"But what about after everything is in the can, we'll still need a Host which would involve hiring a writer?"

I cannot believe we are having this discussion.

"It is my belief that we would have renewed interest because of this strike," he pauses dabbing the corner of his mouth with a Kleenex, "By the time we are ready for a Host, the strike will be long over."

"You amaze me, Fred. Something to think about."

There was a brief silence and a look on Fred's face that I had not yet seen.

"Not getting *The Big Show* on the air was the biggest disappointment of my career," confessed the veteran.

He somehow felt he failed me.

I put my best face forward and tried to tell him that it was not true and not to think that way when Fred started coughing and couldn't catch his breath.

I ached for him and wanted to turn back time. He started breathing strangely.

"This is no way to live," says the man with the strongest will I'll ever know and adds, "This is all I can do."

"I understand."

I got up to hug him for the last time.

"Don't come to close, I don't want you to catch what I have."

I told him that he could kiss my ass and that I loved him.

"But if you do catch something of mine, let's try and sell it."

I hugged him again. Just like a war-buddy.

And like a father, Fred gently patted my back.

"Now go back to work," says the man who never stops teaching and never stops working.

I saw every inch of Fred's face. The room. The pictures. The moment.

The nurse tapped my shoulder and slowly guided me toward the door.

I made my way to the hallway, not wanting to leave yet not wanting to look back.

"Hey!" Shouts Fred de Cordova. I looked back.

"Catch."

From his bed, he throws an imaginary baseball. I catch it.

"Your turn."

With just his eyes, Fred said goodbye.

> "The only professional difference between Fred de Cordova and myself is that I've directed a Noel Coward play; He's directed Noel Coward."
> ~ Mark Bennett

Fred would always want me to call him and tell him about the things that were going on. The last time we actually spoke, I told him about wanting to pitch a couple of projects to NBC but didn't know *the new guy* and asked, "Would it be okay if I called Rick Ludwin?"

Slowly he replied, "Tell him, *First Choice*."

First choice. I can still hear it.

You honor the Network by pitching them first.

When he entered the Motion Picture Home, the reality of him not even being a phone call away became all too evident.

I did, however, have communication with a caretaker named Veronica Rosenblatt who encouraged me to write as (without her saying it) the time was coming soon and visitation for non-family members was not allowed.

The letter was read to him, and two weeks later, on September 15, 2001, he died of natural causes.

The very next day, I attended a very crowded memorial for one of Fred's dearest and closest friends, Bud Robinson.

I think Fred may have been guiding me as I found what seemed to be the last possible vacancy when who should be at the next table but a handful of Carson's Tonight Show alumni.

Odd symmetry as I heard, "Did you hear about Fred?"

When a montage of Bud's life played out, my heart jumped when a close up appeared of my buddy Fred and his pal Bud.

Those memorable pool parties. . . .

That afternoon I came home to a phone call from the lovely Mrs. Janet de Cordova.

She gave me the honor of pallbearer.

Although he lived a long and larger-than-life life: I cried and didn't stop.

The private funeral was an immediate visual example of how Fred de Cordova worked, played and had a personal effect on six decades worth of individuals. I know he was there, watching and smiling. All of us will miss him.

Everyone at some point has had that person who took the risk to say, "Hey kid, let me show you how it's done."

Then, did you take your risk? To say yes, is exciting and scary.

I've noticed, people will remember who was there in the beginning and from where your cornerstone came.

For me, it was the favor I could never pay back, and a gift I will cherish for a lifetime.

On August 28th, 2001, I wrote:

My Dearest Fred,

I've been wanting to do this for quite some time and have had a strong need to put down on paper a couple things that have been mulling about my brain. I suppose, "thank you," is a good start but in comparison to how I feel, it is considerably inadequate.

I have, have had and will continue to have many great teachers but the one who will always hold the title as number one is you. You, Fred, were there in the beginning and just like you promised, you were with me every step of the way.

One time, you had said to me that not getting what we affectionately call our "Big Show" on the air, was a real disappointment for you in your career. I invite you to see it through my eyes as something that was an extraordinary success.

I do not see it as failure because it gave me an unusual opportunity to work with you in the trenches. Your typical selflessness with time and generosity of your knowledge, gave me a Doctorate in Show Business. You can't put a price on that.

Out of that adversity, I also gained someone I get to call Papa Fred. So to me, "The Big Show," two-fold, is a forty share. I hope you now will feel the same.

I would like to see you sometime soon but until then, know that you are always in my heart and that anything I do I hope will be a reflection of all the priceless things you have taught me.

And if you don't like that you can go fuck yourself.

All the good stuff,

Mark Bennett

Acknowledgements

Mary Louise Gemmill and Writers Ascending Literary Management Company—my own Swifty Lazar. Twelve years ago, Janet de Cordova suggested I write about my experiences I had with her dearly departed Fred. I did so, and *The Big Show* was born. The manuscript went around town and even found it's way to The Big Apple. Many friends of Fred read and enjoyed the manuscript. Then, for ten years it sat in a stack of papers in a closet. You ML, had just finished a script I'd written coincidentally called "The Big Show." In passing, I mentioned that it was an adaptation from a manuscript I had written a long time ago. You wanted to read it, I had to dig for it, and you found a home for it in a day. I signed a contract the day after that. I truly appreciate your enthusiasm and now after all these years, and because of you, other people will have a chance to learn a little extra about Fred.

Larry Czerwonka, my Publisher, I truly appreciate how you treated the story. You "got" the tempo of the piece and more importantly, you genuinely "got" Fred. Thank you for being my first "fast-track" experience. I'm still catching my breath.

Ted Melfi and Kimberly Quinn, our dear neighbors and friends. We have always been cheerleaders for each other but I wanted to thank you for opening up your whole family so much so that they feel like ours too. Thank you Ted for introducing me to your brother Phil.

The late Phil Melfi. Phil was a partner for a little magazine called *Screenwriter's Monthly*. He read the manuscript and told me, "I want my life to be like this." He printed excerpts of it in his Hollywood rag. He was there first, ten years ago, and I'm sure he's in Heaven right now talking Fred's ear off.

Joe Dera, my publicist from back in the day. You graciously read my manuscript and asked if you could send it to your friend, Jann Wenner of *Rolling Stone* magazine. It was a tough decision but I still let you do it. I remember Mr. Wenner telling you he liked it but it was the kind of piece they did 30 years ago. So, no *Rolling Stone* but thanks anyway.

To all the individuals mentioned in the story, clearly you all made a deep impression on me, I learned a lot and that opportunity gave me the problems of someone twice my age. You all were my teachers. Thank you.

Mom and Dad, I know it was very hard for you to get your heads around the fact that your child, barely out of college and doing black box theatre in LA suddenly had a title, an office and an assistant. And you would call my office and tell her to make sure I call collect. You were two states away in a pre-Google world. I hope by reading this story you will see what a protector Fred was for your son in this crazy town. Thank you for your genes and solid upbringing. Michael Bennett, my big brother, it really happened. I love you. And Grams, I think of you every day.

Thank you Danny Robinson, David Tenzer, Alix Hartley, Roger Strull, Todd Leavitt, Leslie Abell, Bob Dolan Smith, Courtney Conte, Steve Schifrin, Randy Haberkamp, Kenny Ortega, Dee Baker, Don Sweeney, Helen Sanders, Stephanie Ross, Sandy Varga, Teresa Ledesma, Karen Fogerty, Marsha Goodman, Irvin Arthur, Noah Fogelson, Gary Pudney, Shirlee Fonda, Dick Martin, Freddie Fields, Arthur Price, Bill Robinson, Susie Allen, Ron Revier, Carol Wickham, The Kellers, Derek Parks, Chuck Harlow, J. Scott Hardman, David Johnson and Deanna, The Haffleys, The Fails, The Elders, The Dempseys and Bob Newhart.

Mark Bennett currently lives in Los Angeles with his wife and newly adopted cat who strangely came with the name, Freddie. This story is for all the mentors (in any industry) who selflessly share what they know and change the way we receivers think.

Photo by Greg Crowder

markbennettauthor.com

Made in the USA
Charleston, SC
18 February 2014